THIS IS LIFE ETERNAL

Why Many Christians Will Not Make Heaven

Bill Fonte

Ranell Publishing
Keller, Texas

This Is Life Eternal:
Why Many Christians Will Not Make Heaven

Copyright © 2007 by Bill Fonte
All rights reserved
Printed in the United States of America
International Standard Book Number: 978-0-9819067-0-6
Library of Congress Catalog Card Number: 2009922837

Published by Ranell Publishing
P.O. Box 207
Keller, TX. 76244

Direct inquires to the above address
or e-mail to info@ranellpublishing.com

Cover design by Lamb Creek Created Services
Peter Lamb
www.lambcreek.com

CONTENTS

ACKNOWLEDGMENTS

This book is dedicated to the Glory of God and for his praise and exaltation. This could not have been accomplished without the help of my beautiful wife, Ranell, and our dear friend, Elita Driskill. They both worked together with me in presenting the Word of God to Christ's body of believers. With many hours and much determination, in addition to their regular full time jobs, they labored in helping me put this book together.

God bless you both.

INTRODUCTION

This book is written to exhort individuals to awaken to the truth about eternal life. Inspired by the Word of God and the Spirit of God, this exhortation is given to awaken many and prepare them for the return of the Lord Jesus Christ. The Lord Jesus himself stated in Matthew 7:21, "Not everyone that saith unto me, Lord, Lord, shall enter into the kingdom of heaven; but he that doeth the will of my Father which is in heaven."

The time grows closer for his return. It is time to prepare and be ready by receiving and walking in this eternal life that he has given to us. I pray your mind and heart will be open to receive what the Lord is saying through these words and to not walk in the things of man but in the things of God.

WHAT IS ETERNAL LIFE?

Do you want to live forever in heaven? What are the requirements for getting there? Is it enough to be a good person or to live a certain lifestyle? Most people asking these questions, and even those who are answering them, are often so unsure of themselves that they speculate or simply hope that they will end up in heaven. Fortunately, though, the Bible has the answers to all these questions.

The Word of God tells us in James 4:14 that the life we are living is only "a vapor that appears for a little while and then vanishes away." Just lean over to someone near you and blow in their ear. That small breath was equivalent to the life you will live here on the earth when you compare it to eternity. The one thing we are counting on, though, is that the way we are living here on earth during this brief whisper will eventually grant us an entrance or a qualification to have eternal life in heaven.

What exactly is eternal life? What does it mean to live forever? Well, the "eternal" part is easy to understand. It means forever, without end, no stopping, always continuing, etc. The "life" part is where most people fall short in understanding. We are actually spirit beings living in an earthly body. We are eternal, made in the likeness of God, who is eternal. We are not earthly beings trying to be spiritual - we are a spirit living in an earthly body. When we die physically, our spirit will be separated from our body, but it will still live on forever. We will all still exist eternally, but some will have eternal life and others will have eternal death.

Jesus actually gave a definition for eternal life in John 17:3 (KJV). After he stated "this is life eternal", he explained that it is to know the only true God and Jesus Christ whom he sent. So, how do I know if I know God and Jesus Christ? Since this is what eternal life is all about, then I must know them both to have it.

The word "know" in the actual Greek is Ginosko, and according to W.E. Vine's An Expository Dictionary Of New Testament Words, it means to be taking in knowledge, to come to know, recognize, understand, or to understand completely. Here in John 17:3, it indicates a relationship between the person knowing and the object being known. In this respect, what is known is of value or importance to the one who knows it. He goes on to say that this knowledge or knowing is gained not by intellectual activity but by operation of the Holy Spirit, and this knowing is increasing all the time. If we know God and Jesus, then they are the most important and the most valuable individuals in our lives. What they tell us is the most important and the most valuable information in our lives. Whoever is valuable and important to us will take first place in our lives, and we will give up everything necessary to please them. What they say will be more important than what someone else says. We will be committed to them and their Words as we grow and increase in our knowledge of them. Do you know the Lord? In Titus, the Apostle Paul warns us of deceivers who will declare they know God, but in their works they actually deny him. In I John chapter 4, he refers to those who have been born of God as the ones who know and love God. Knowing your Lord is the most important thing you can do to make sure of your eternity.

According to the Lord Jesus, many will have eternal damnation or eternal death. In Luke 13:24 (KJV), the Lord said to "Strive to enter in at the strait gate: for many, I say unto you, will seek to enter in, and shall not be able." Eternal death actually means to be separated from God forever. When someone dies naturally, they are separated from their body. They still exist somewhere else. Eternal death, then, is to be separated forever from love, joy, peace, goodness, kindness, patience, faith, meekness, self control, health, and the list goes on and on. Eternal death is separation from every characteristic of God - forever. To never again experience His presence or His mercy or His love would be separation from the life of God, or the God kind of life.

Some jokingly talk about spending eternity with their buddies, living it up and having a great time in hell. There have been movies where people would say "See you in hell" and act as though it really is no big deal. But, hell is eternal suffering – suffering forever. There is no escape. It is final. There are no second or third chances. People in hell are separated from all joy and peace and goodness. There is no kindness in hell. Only evil beings dwell there and its inhabitants suffer forever. There is no laughter or anything that feels good. There is no good time. There is only sorrow, grief, and pain constantly. The Lord Jesus referred to some of this in Matthew 24:51 and Matthew 25:30 - there is weeping and gnashing of teeth. In Luke 16 he talks about the rich man in hell, and he called it a place of torment. In the original Greek, this word indicates pain, loss, toil, tossing, and torture. Everyone there will hate each other and will hate being there, yet they will be there for eternity without any way to escape. How do we avoid this place? How do we get this eternal life instead of eternal death? How can we be with God forever? How can we avoid being absent from God for eternity?

Many ministers have been asked by bereaved loved ones to assure them that a deceased friend or relative is in paradise or heaven. The minister is expected to ease their conscience by saying that everything is okay and their loved ones are at rest in heaven with God - regardless of how they lived their life on earth. We have come to base our eternal life status on what the "man of God" tells us rather than what the Word of God says, which is that very few will go to heaven.

Of course, no one knows the heart of man except God. But he has given us his Word so we can know for sure how to obtain eternal life. According to John in I John 5:13, "These things I have written to you who believe in the name of the Son of God, that you may know that you have eternal life, and that you may continue to believe in the name of the Son of God." What things did John write? We will look at them later.

When the Lord Jesus said that He came so we could have abundant life (John 10:10), what kind of life was he talking about? Was He referring to material things or spiritual things? According to a variety of preachers during the past 20 years, it might appear that it is material things. That is the wrong answer! The Lord Jesus said in Luke 12:15, "for one's life does not consist in the abundance of the things he possesses." In other words, life is not about what you have materially. It is also mentioned in I Timothy 6:5 that some think that "godliness is a means of gain" for material possessions. Paul said to withdraw from these people. Instead, most of the body of Christ flocks around these people. Why? The reason is simply greed for money and possessions. This type of teaching is also against godliness. Paul stresses again that godliness with contentment is great gain.

I recently heard someone say that you cannot be in perfect peace unless all of your bills are paid. This man's peace is evidently based upon how much money he has or how many possessions he has. It is based upon having a material possession and not a spiritual one. Many people think that having money equates to the perfect peace that God gives. That is why the Word tells us that many have "pierced themselves through with many sorrows" because they travel this pathway of belief (I Timothy 6:10). They believe that money is what gives them joy and love and peace. The material things they own are what gives them comfort and tranquility. Watch people when they lose possessions and things of this earth. See what happens to them and how their attitudes change about life. See if they lose that zeal and spunk they had when everything was going great. If they do, then they are going after money and possessions more than the life that God has come to give us.

According to Isaiah 26:3, perfect peace comes from God, the life-giver, and we should keep our minds centered or focused on him. You can be the poorest person on the face of this earth monetarily, and still have perfect peace and the life of God inside of you. If you became poor and lost everything you owned, would you still have the peace of God? Would you still be excited about eternal life and the God who gave it to you?

The life the Lord talked about is found only through Him. In 1 John 5:12 it says, "He who has the Son has life; he who does not have the Son of God does not have life." The Lord Jesus is the life-giver. In John 17:2, Jesus said that the Father has given him authority over all flesh, and that Jesus should give eternal life to all that the Father has given him. God's life is full of love, joy, peace, mercy, forgiveness, kindness, patience, goodness, meekness, self control, and all good things. This life only comes through Jesus Christ. In Galatians 5:22-23, the Apostle Paul calls it the fruit of the Spirit. In other words, this is what should be coming out of people's lives that are believers in Jesus Christ.

In Mathew 6:33, the Lord Jesus said to "seek first the kingdom of God and His righteousness, and all these things shall be added to you". Seek what first? Seek the kingdom of God first. The Word of God tells us in Romans 14:17 that the kingdom of

God is not about eating and drinking (material things), but righteousness, peace, and joy (spiritual things) in the Holy Spirit. Yes, we do need material things to live here on the Earth. God supplies these things to everyone. In James 1:5, the Word of God tells us that God gives to all men liberally and does it without finding fault. We are to seek HIM who is the giver of life and not the THINGS on this earth.

If we have been raised with Christ, we are to seek those things that are above, where Christ sits at the right hand of the Father (Colossians 3:1-2). We are to set our mind on the things above and not on the things of earth. Where are your thoughts each day? Are they on the things above where Jesus the Lord is sitting, or are they on the things of this earth? Notice it tells us to SET our minds on the things above. When cement is poured, it has to SET to become firm and solid. Your mind needs to become solid and unmoved in thinking on the things above and not on the things of the earth. When Joshua was taking over to lead the children of Israel into the Promised Land (Joshua 1), God told him to make sure he kept his mind focused or centered on God's Word. He was not to look to the left or to the right, but to keep focused on the Word. He was to make sure he read it, spoke it, and meditated on it daily, and then did what it said to do. This practice would cause him to be successful and prosperous.

THE WAY TO ETERNAL LIFE

Why does life come only from Jesus Christ and not from some other person or by another way? You will find that every other way to eternal life is about trying to be good. The theme seems to be that if the good deeds done in life out-weigh the bad deeds, you should make it to eternal life. Just be a good ol' boy, be good to everyone, follow the rules, and you will make it to Heaven. What standard is that based on? What foundation makes that statement true?

Many people have no idea at all how to obtain eternal life. Some rely on beliefs that are different from God's Word, simply because that is what they have been told by others. Some form their own opinions based on their life experiences. Most believe that whatever feels good to them or fits into their world-view is what will lead to eternal life. How sad to know that so many are following such pathways, but all of these pathways lead to eternal death. Jesus Christ told his followers in John 14:1 "you believe in God, believe also in me." In other words, if you are committed to God, then commit your life to Jesus Christ also.

Jesus then told them in the next two verses of John 14 that he was going away to build them homes in his Father's house. He told them that when he was finished, he would come back again and get them. He then said in verse four, "where I go you know, and the way you know." One of the followers said, "we do not know where You are going, and how can we know the way?" Jesus answered him in verse six, "I am the way, the truth, and the life. No one comes to the Father except through me."

Jesus Christ is the only way to get to the Father, the only way to get to God, the only way to get to heaven, and the only way to have eternal life. He is the only One that came down to the earth, shed his blood and died on the cross for the forgiveness of our sins. No one else has sacrificed their life for you. The Lord Jesus took our place on the cross and was separated from God. When he was on that cross, he cried out to his Father, "Why have You forsaken Me?" (Matthew 27:46) He was separated so we would not have to be. If you are separated from God, you will receive eternal damnation, eternal death.

Not only did Jesus Christ die for our sins, but God the Father raised him up from the dead. He now lives forever, waiting for us to accept his sacrifice and receive this eternal life. If you repent of your way of living and commit to these words and to the Lord Jesus Christ to follow him, then you will receive the work he did for you and all of mankind.

You will receive the forgiveness of your sins and eternal life. This only comes through Jesus Christ, who paid the price for your salvation and grants you entrance into the kingdom of heaven by your believing in him and being born again. If you insist on your own way of living that is contrary to following the ways of Jesus Christ, then you will be separated from Him forever in hell.

The Lord Jesus said in John 3:3 that a man cannot enter into the kingdom of heaven unless he is born again. That which is born of water and the Spirit will enter the kingdom of heaven. How is one born of the Spirit? It requires a change. The Lord said in verse eight that it is like the wind that blows - you hear it and feel it, but you do not know where it comes from or where it is going. Many people try to enter this eternal life without changing on the inside. It cannot be done. The Lord said you MUST be born again. To be born again is like actually starting over brand new. Everything in your past is forgiven and forgotten; everything in your life now becomes brand new. This is done in your heart by the Spirit of God. It requires conviction of the sin in your life after hearing His words. You now realize all the sinful things you are doing and that everything he says is right.

Proverbs 14:12 tells us that there is a way that seems good to man, but it is the way of death.

Why follow a pathway that leads to death? If you try to enter eternal life by any way other than Jesus Christ, it is a way that leads to eternal death. If you were traveling down a highway in your car and knew that if you stayed on that highway you would die, then you would turn around and go the other way. Yet so many people are on the wrong road and they do not know it is leading to death. Even many who call themselves Christians are on the wrong road. They think they have believed on Jesus, but they have formed their own way about believing in him. They have made their own way and that way leads to death.

Many people are traveling a road that they believe will lead to eternal life. If you did a survey and asked them if they are going to heaven when they die, most would answer that they believe so, or they hope so. When you ask them what they base that answer on, you truly find out what they believe. Even then, you have to be careful with your question because many people have learned to give the right answer without living the right way. Some live life way out of control and others live in a very religious manner, yet still most think they are going to live forever with God. Jesus said he is the WAY, the TRUTH, and the LIFE. In order to have the right LIFE, you must live the right WAY according to the right TRUTH.

THE NARROW ROAD

The Lord Jesus said in Matthew 7:13-14 that the way to eternal life is hard and narrow and few will find it, but the way to destruction is broad and many are on that road. In Luke 13:23 someone asked Jesus, "are there few who are saved?" He replied, "Strive to enter through the narrow gate, for many, I say to you, will seek to enter and will not be able." He said that once the door is shut to eternal life, many will say "Lord, Lord, open up to us" and He will tell them "I know you not." How is it that they can call him Lord, but he will not let them in? The Word of God says in 1 Corinthians 12:3 that "no one can say that Jesus is Lord except by the Holy Spirit." In Romans 10:9 the Word of God tells us that "if you confess with your mouth the Lord Jesus and believe in your heart that God has raised him from the dead, you will be saved." They had to have known him at one time to be able to call him Lord. These people must think they really know Him, yet according to the Lord Jesus they do not. How sad to think that many people who think that they are following the way of Jesus are actually following another pathway. The end of that other pathway cannot be eternal life. They will live eternally without life, being separated from the one they thought they were following. They evidently were following a WAY that was easy and wide. The road to eternal life is a very difficult road, according to the Word of God. It is very tight and very narrow and few find it. Living your own way or however you think is right that is against God's Word is the broad and easy road, and it leads to destruction.

In John 10:1, Jesus said that those who try to enter the sheepfold by another way are thieves and robbers. What way could these people who called him Lord be following? What TRUTH were they listening to? Jesus said in John 10:27, "My sheep hear My voice, and I know them, and they follow Me." Again he uses the word "know." There must be something significant about that word. In Luke 13:26 they tell him that they have eaten and drunk in his presence and he has taught them in their streets. They evidently were in the presence of his words and his ways. The Lord then tells them in verse 27, "I do not know you, where you are from. Depart from Me, all you workers of iniquity." That word "iniquity" means to live a life of lawlessness - a life lived doing less than what the law requires. Imagine the feeling and the look on people's faces who think they are on their way to eternal life with Jesus when they suddenly find out that He does not know them. The Lord said in verse 28 that there will be weeping and gnashing of teeth when they are thrust out of the kingdom. You have to be in the kingdom first before you can be thrust out of it later.

It will happen because they did not follow the right WAY or the TRUTH or the LIFE.

In Mathew 7:21 the Lord Jesus said, "Not everyone who says to me, 'Lord, Lord,' shall enter the kingdom of heaven, but he who does the will of My Father in heaven." In verse 23 he tells them again, "I never knew you; depart from Me, you who practice lawlessness!" What is the will of God? Jesus said he who does it is the one who enters into eternal life. Let us see what God considers to be his will.

There was a man who came to Jesus in Mathew 19:16 and asked, "What good thing shall I do that I may have eternal life?" Jesus told him that if he wants to enter into life then he should keep the commandments. The man then asked which commandments he had to keep. Isn't it like man to try to pick and choose which ones he wants to live by instead of living by all of them? We try to pick and choose our way into heaven by keeping what we want and not what God tells us. The Lord gave him an answer and the man replied that he had kept these commandments from his youth. Jesus knew the man's heart and the pathway his life was traveling. He knew the man was on the pathway of possessions and greed. He told the man to go and sell all that he had and give it to the poor, and then to follow Jesus. The man walked away sad because he had great wealth. Jesus said the same thing in Mathew 16:24, "If anyone desires to come after Me, let him deny himself, and take up his cross, and follow me."

Jesus made a statement that should send tremors throughout all of Christianity. He said in Matthew 19:23, "It is hard for a rich man to enter the kingdom of heaven". We know that Jesus meant that those who trust in their riches will not be able to enter in. In Mathew 7:20, he tells us that these people are known by their fruits. If you have listened to much preaching over the last twenty years, you have probably heard a number of people claim to call Jesus their Lord, and yet put their trust in money. The Lord does provide for us by allowing us to make money on our jobs and meeting our needs. The Lord Jesus also said to make friends with our unrighteous mammon or wealth by giving it to the poor and needy. What an awesome sight it would be to see ministries giving money away to those with needs instead of always asking for more money and promising riches in return! Most of Christianity has fallen into the trap of wanting to be rich. In 1 Timothy 6:8, we are told to be content with simply having food and clothing. The writer of Hebrews in chapter 13 verse 5 tells us to let our way of living be without covetousness and to be content with what we have. Money should be used by Christianity to establish and preach the gospel of

Jesus Christ. One of the most effective ways to reach others is one-on-one evangelism. But the role of the missionary has been forgotten and their financial support has been neglected by the Christian community. Instead, financial support many times goes to other ministries that promise selfish gain in return. The Word of God tells me to seek first the kingdom of God and his righteousness, and all the things I have need of shall be met. What a contrast.

When did someone come to the Lord Jesus asking for a need to be met, only to be told they had to give something first? How often do we hear that if we just send in a certain amount of money, we will have our needs met? How often are we promised that the anointing will increase in our life if we will just give money to support this ministry or that one? Why do we think the things of God can be purchased? The Lord said to believe in Him, not in our money. If we know the will of God and do it, then He will make sure all of our needs are met.

Jesus told the man in Mathew 19:21 to give up everything to get eternal life. Modern man says to give up everything to get riches. I wonder what WAY is correct. What TRUTH are we to follow? Peter told the Lord Jesus in John 6:68 that he, Jesus, had the words of eternal life. Whose words are you listening to? Whose words are you following? If you do the words of Jesus then you are on the right pathway. What road are you following? What pathway do you seek? Is it narrow and tight or is your way broad?

In Luke 16:19-31 the Lord Jesus tells us a story. This is not a parable, but a true story. He tells us that there was a certain rich man who was dressed very well and lived in luxury every day. There was a certain beggar named Lazarus which stayed in front of the rich man's house and begged to be allowed to eat the crumbs that fell from the rich man's table. This beggar was full of sores, and the dogs came and licked them. When both of these individuals died, one went to eternal life and the other went to eternal death. What made the difference? Both called Abraham their father. They both had a covenant with God through Father Abraham. They were both evidently in the family of God. What made the difference? Why did one end up in hell and the other in heaven? It was because the rich man did not help the poor man. He was concerned only about himself. He had been given good things and he did not use them for the kingdom of God by helping those who were poor.

It is amazing how we can be so led astray by those who call themselves Christians, yet many attempt to make merchandise of us with their deceptive words as described in 2 Peter 2:3.

Through their greed, they preach deceptive words in order to get your money. Paul asked the church at Galatia who had bewitched them so that they did not obey the truth (Galatians 3:1). What happened to the Church at Galatia is what has happened to many churches in America and throughout the world. They have wandered away from the Truth. That is why the Lord said in Mathew 7:21 that many will come to Him in that day and call Him "Lord, Lord" but will not make heaven. He said he did not know them. They had moved away from the truth of God's word and had gone after teachers who would scratch their ears with things they wanted to hear, according to what they wanted or lusted for (2 Timothy4:3-4). Many do not want to hear that the road to heaven is tight and narrow and hard to follow. They want to hear it is full of ease and God will bless you every step of the way with ease and comfort.

In Matthew 7:14 (KJV), the Lord Jesus said that "...strait is the gate, and narrow is the way..." that leads to eternal life. The word "strait" (in the original Greek) means to suffer affliction, to be troubled, or to suffer due to the pressure of circumstances or the antagonism of people. The word "narrow" (in the original Greek) means to be hemmed in like a mountain gorge. It is a very tight spot to enter. So if the gate to get in to eternal life is full of sufferings due to pressure and the way is a very tight spot to go through, that does not sound like ease and comfort! Today's Christianity makes it sound so easy and comfortable, yet it is full of suffering and very hard to get in. The Lord said in Luke 13:26-27 that many will seek to enter in and will not be able to. You literally have to suffer the loss of all things, including yourself, to have eternal life. Life is not about you, but about the Lord. It is about knowing him and giving up everything to know him even more. Many people have had to literally give up their physical life because they believed in Jesus. Many have been forsaken by their families, been tortured, and had everything taken away from them. The entrance is full of pressure and the way is very tight.

In John 6:27-29 the Lord Jesus tells us to "not labor for the food which perishes, but for the food which endures to everlasting life." Do not labor for things that will fall away and perish with time. Do not let that be what is important in your life. As we said earlier, the Lord told us that life does not consist in the abundance of the things you possess. He said do not put that first in your life.

I was in a church service one evening and the preacher challenged all the church members to put God first during the first week of the New Year by fasting, praying, and studying his word. He even talked about giving up entertainment like listening to music or watching TV and movies. I thought God is supposed to be first every day of our lives and not just the first week of the year? I thought we should be seeking his kingdom first every day and not just one week out of the year? The sad part about his challenge to the congregation was that he laughed and said that it would be okay to watch the Dallas Cowboys, though, since they were in the playoffs – just abstain from other television shows. The Lord said in Mathew 6:21 that you can tell where your heart is by looking at what you treasure. Is football your treasure? What is it that stands in the way of your doing everything the Lord is telling you to do?

What is your treasure? What do you value and pursue first in your life? What excites you when you wake up in the morning? What excites you throughout the day? Do you get more joy and excitement from receiving money than you do when you hear from the Lord with a directive to make a sacrifice or love your enemy? What do you talk about most? Is it the current events of the day? Is it the latest sports stories? Are you more excited about the American Idol? Or are you excited to talk and hear about the Lord Jesus? You will find your heart going after whatever your treasure is. To some it is the world of sports, money, possessions, religion, etc. To those who truly know Him, it is the pursuit of God and Jesus Christ.

In John 6:27-29 Jesus told us to work for the food that does not perish – for eternal life from the Son of Man. The people asked Jesus what they must do to work the works of God. In other words, where should we be laboring or working? The Lord told them that the work of God is simply that you "believe in Him whom He sent." Believe on Jesus Christ and you will be working the works of God. You will be doing his will. Believe what? Believe everything he said and do it. That is why he told them in Matthew 7:24 that whoever hears his sayings and does them is a wise man. Notice the heart is found where its treasure is. In other words, since it is the heart where man believes (Romans 10:10), then what we believe is important and is where our treasure is. That word "believe" (in the original Greek) means to commit to trust. Our treasure will be whatever we believe in or commit to trust in. What do most people believe or commit to? If you read Mathew 6:32-33, the Lord said to not worry about the things you need because he knows you have need of them. He then told us to "seek first the kingdom of God and His righteousness", and everything you have need of will be given to you. Notice he did not say to give to people so you can be blessed with material things.

He said to seek first the kingdom of God. In Romans 14:17 we read earlier that the kingdom of God is not about eating and drinking (material things), but righteousness, peace, and joy (spiritual things) in the Holy Spirit. Food that produces Eternal Life is spiritual. What a contrast to what we hear preached by many ministries. Are you committed to the Word of the Lord? Are you showing love to your enemies? Are you doing good things for those who hate you? Are you praying for those who spitefully use you and persecute you? Are you committed to every Word of God, or just the ones you want to live by? What you are committed to and Who you know will determine if you will live forever in heaven or in hell.

Does spending time in prayer and in the Word of God excite you? Do you prefer to give things away or to receive them? The Word of God tells us it is more blessed to give than to receive. If you seek the will and Word of God, you will not have to be concerned about things. Just believe on what the Lord Jesus Christ is telling you and showing you and follow that. You will not hear it, though, unless you are seeking his kingdom. He should be first place in everything you do and say. Hear from him yourself and do not rely on someone to hear for you. If you are born again, listen to hear the voice of God. He will talk to you and lead you in the way to go. He will lead you in the way of his Word. If you are not born again, then seek the Lord with all your heart and do not stop until you are made brand new.

Paul prayed in Philippians 3:10 that he wanted to know Christ, but he first said he counted everything he had ever done or achieved as dung. All Paul wanted was Christ. He couldn't care less if he had money or things because he knew they were temporary and soon to pass away. Knowing Jesus to him was life eternal. It sounds like the road to eternal life is pretty tough.

Remember the Lord told those people in Mathew 7 that he did not know them because they were workers of iniquity. They were doing less than what the law required. Someone in our society who was driving a motor vehicle and constantly ran red lights would be someone who did less than the law requires. God has a law that every person who calls themselves a Christian should be following. That is the royal law of love. The Word tells us in Matthew 22:37 that the greatest of all the commandments is to love the Lord your God with all your heart, soul, and mind. Are you doing that? In verse 39, he said the second greatest commandment is to love your neighbor as yourself. Are you doing that? Is love what excites you and motivates you every day? Paul said in 1 Corinthians 14:1 (amplified version) that we are to eagerly pursue this love and let this love be our great quest and aim in life. Is it? Are you seeking to know and walk in the God kind of love? The Spirit of God will always lead you to walk in his love in every situation and toward every individual.

Most people, though, are more concerned about themselves than about showing the love of God. They are more concerned about collecting possessions than about loving others. Jesus said in John 14:15 that if we love Him we will keep his commands or words. In 1 John 2:3-4 the Word says that the way we are sure that we know him is if we keep his words. It says that those who say they know him but do not keep his words are liars! Evidently the people working iniquity in Mathew 7 were not walking in love and were not keeping the commands of the Lord. They evidently went to church because they drank and ate in his presence, but they must not have practiced his Word in their daily life. They must not have walked in love to others and to God. Do you call him 'Lord, Lord?' Are you one of the many who attend church but do not practice his commands?

The Ephesian church in Revelation 2 was told how many good works they were doing for Jesus. But he also told them he had one thing against them. They had left their first love. He told them to repent and do the first works or else they would be removed as his church. Notice the first love is considered a work and that if you leave it you are in danger of being removed from his church. Do you see why walking in love is so important?

In Mathew 25 the Lord tells us what will happen before his Throne of Glory in verses 31-46. He will gather all nations and will separate them like a shepherd divides his sheep and goats, with the sheep on his right and the goats on his left. He will say to the sheep, "Come, you blessed of my Father, inherit the kingdom prepared for you from the foundation of the world." Why are they allowed to come into the kingdom? He said, "for I was hungry and you gave Me food; I was thirsty and you gave Me drink; I was a stranger and you took Me in; I was naked and you clothed Me; I was sick and you visited Me; I was in prison and you came to Me." They called him Lord and asked when it was that they did these things. Notice they called him Lord. He went on to tell them that when they did it for the least of their brethren they actually did it for Jesus. He then told the goats on his left to depart from him into everlasting fire prepared for the devil and his angels. He told them "I was hungry and you gave Me no food, I was thirsty and you gave Me no drink, I was a stranger and you did not take Me in; naked and you did not clothe Me, sick and in prison and you did not visit Me." Notice, then, that they also called him Lord and asked when they did these things. They evidently were members of a church somewhere because they called him Lord. These people were sent to everlasting punishment but the righteous were sent to everlasting life. What made the difference? They were both calling Him LORD, but they were not all obeying his commands.

The theme in pulpits today is one of ease and comfort. There is very little mention of repentance and change. All many people know is that they simply repeated a prayer as they were led and now they are Christians because that is what they were told. There was no change of heart and no change of lifestyle. I cannot count how many times I have met people who are not living for Christ and yet call themselves Christians. They call Jesus Lord and are not doing the things he has told them. The Lord said in Luke 6:46, "But why do you call me 'Lord, Lord,' and not do the things which I say?" How many Christians are not living the life Jesus said we would live if we BELIEVE in Him. Remember that word "believe" means to "commit to trust". If we have believed on Jesus, then we are committed to his words and his way and his truth. Our desire should be to do everything he tells us in his Word. If you are not following his truth, now is the time to repent (turn around) and begin following his narrow path. Become a sheep and not a goat. Are you loving him by keeping his words or are you doing what you want and how you want? Your eternity depends on who or what you are committed to. Has someone tricked you like the Galatian church – are you looking at things rather than at Jesus? Don't let pride stand in your way. Godly sorrow will work repentance and

will produce salvation. It is God you must someday
stand before, not an earthly minister. The road
leading to eternal life is tough. It requires all of us
to give up everything to follow Jesus.

LOVE, THE MOST EXCELLENT WAY

Mathew 5:44 tells us to love our enemies. How can someone love their enemy? The Lord said to "bless those who curse you, do good to those who hate you, and pray for those who spitefully use you and persecute you." I can assure you that many people all over the United States have grandparents and great grandparents who have shown an incredible lack of love for certain minority groups over the years. We were all minorities in this nation at one point, yet according to our nation's history we have failed miserably in loving one another. The South was supposed to be the Bible Belt of our nation! You would have never known it the way Christian brothers and sisters treated each other.

Brother Martin Luther King preached the truth about walking in love, and yet many did not heed the Word of God coming from his mouth. They chose hate instead. Most that chose that path even called themselves Christians. The prejudice and hatred of that day still exists in many who call themselves Christians today. Again, the words of our Lord Jesus ring true, "many will come to me in that day and say Lord, Lord."

James 2:1-9 tells us to not have the faith of our Lord Jesus Christ with respect of persons. If you judge someone based on their appearance and clothing, then you have become the judge of evil thoughts and you commit sin. In other words, your thoughts judge people and their actions, based on their appearance. How many times does that happen in our daily living with people we meet? I am amazed at all the whispers I get from people when they choose not to speak their prejudices out loud. They don't want others to hear them. Do they not realize that the Lord is listening to every word they speak? He said the mouth speaks out of the abundance of the heart. If we speak prejudice, it is within our heart.

James teaches us to have the faith of Jesus without prejudice. If we treat people differently because of what they wear or what they do or who they are or the color of their skin or how they act, then we have prejudice. I am amazed at the people who call themselves Christians and yet have prejudice towards people who are different from themselves. Years ago, there was so much prejudice towards the African Americans in this country. Even still today there are often remarks made about them, as well as many other ethnic groups. These jokes and comments are being spoken by people who call themselves Christians.

During the civil rights movement, many who called themselves Christians made their voices known by their actions. They went to church every Sunday but still hated the black man. They were so deceived. Going to church does not make you a Christian any more than going to a fast food restaurant makes you a hamburger. Christians are known by their love – the love of Christ.

I went to court one day to defend myself when I was accused of running a red light. The bottom line was that it was simply my word against the officer's word. The prosecuting attorney said that there was no evidence, yet the jury declared me guilty. I was so shocked that they would take his word over mine without evidence! But the police officer's position gave his words more weight than mine. In James 2:1-9 we are told that if we pick one person over another based on their dress or position, then we show prejudice and sin. How many times do people walk that way and yet they tell everyone that they are on their way to heaven.

There was a man who attended my bible study years ago that had such hatred for homosexuals. He detested their lifestyle and made it a point to slur them every chance he could. He hated to see them flaunt their ways on TV. One day he had some problems and needed counseling. He went to group therapy and guess which member of his group was sitting right next to him? It was a man who practiced homosexuality! During the sessions of counseling, he listened to this man and realized that they were both just people with problems. He realized how this man needed to repent and turn his life to Jesus so he could have eternal life. He began to show compassion for this man even though he hated his lifestyle. Many Christians today have similar prejudices. They may show it in different ways and to different groups, but it is the same sin. It even exists in Christian circles regarding denomination. Why don't the Assembly of God churches have guest Baptist preachers? Why don't the Methodist churches have guest Episcopalian preachers? Why don't the Catholic churches have guest Charismatic preachers? Why don't the Baptist churches have guest Word of Faith preachers? Why doesn't the Church of Christ denomination invite Catholics to preach? The answer is very easy to see. They have respect of persons and sin. These groups boast about what wonderful works they are doing, yet they don't even show the love of Christ toward each other. Instead, they show prejudice.

Getting remarried after being divorced makes you unfit to preach in some denominations. I wonder how these denominations explain the story in John 4:7-30 where Jesus met the woman at the well. The Lord Jesus began to tell her things about herself and about eternal life. This woman had been divorced five times and was currently living in fornication (this practice is not new to the 20th century)! After she realized who the Lord was, she went back to her own city and told them (preached) about Jesus. According to some denominations, she should not have been allowed to tell about Jesus because she had been married to more than one man. Why did the Lord Jesus not have a problem with this? We are told in the Word of God (2 Timothy 2:21) that if we cleanse ourselves, we will then be a "vessel for honor, sanctified and useful for the Master."

Don't let the prejudice toward anyone make your love wax cold. Forgive them and love them! I encourage you to let go of any prejudices toward others if they exist. Pray for them and love them! We all have to stand before the Lord one day and give an account of what we have done. It won't be worth it to spend eternity in hell because of prejudices.

I once heard about a young Christian man who strayed from the truth while trying to make his point about abortion clinics being wrong. According to God's Word, he is supposed to love his enemies. Instead, he blew up an abortion clinic and killed the doctor inside. Why? This man said he was inspired by Christian radio! Of course, he was not encouraged to do exactly that deed, but his hatred and prejudice were encouraged. The hatred or prejudice can turn our hearts from what we believe to be right to an act of sin. Don't let yourself be led astray like the Galatians! The Galatian church heard the truth and decided to live life differently than what was preached to them.

Years ago I believe the Lord tested the church in this nation when President Bill Clinton was in office. He was caught in the act of adultery. He denied it at first and then confessed it later. A number of preachers and so-called Christian talk show hosts spoke their hatred across America, and I believe it was a stink in the nostrils of God. Yes, the President did wrong and he was guilty. Yes, he should have been removed from office for his actions. But the reaction from people who called themselves Christians was appalling. Where was love? Where was prayer? In 1 Timothy 2:1-4 we are told to pray for those in authority over us. People were throwing verbal stones at him left and right. Imagine if your sin was broadcast all over America and everyone knew about it. Would you want to be "stoned" or would you prefer love and prayer? The people who call Jesus Lord must act and live according to what his words tell us. That is supposed to be what sets Christians apart from the rest of the world.

Jesus is our greatest example, so let's look at the story of a woman caught in the act of adultery in

John 8:3-11. The people brought her to Jesus and told him what the Word of God (the law given to Moses) said concerning her act of sin. Listen carefully to what he tells us by his actions in this situation. He told the crowd that anybody who had no sin could throw the first stone at her. They all left without throwing any stones. Jesus then told her that he did not condemn her and that she was to go and sin no more. But the Word according to Moses was that she should be stoned. Why didn't he have her stoned? This is the Son of the living God who does no wrong! Jesus was teaching us here that we are to live by the Spirit of the Word, and not just by the letter of the law. Some want to say that they live according to God's Word, but they deny him in their actions. They deny him by their lack of love.

The disciples were walking with Jesus on the road to Jerusalem one day and they decided to stop at Samaria. The Samaritans saw they were headed to Jerusalem and told them they did not want them there. The disciples were rejected for who they were and what their purpose or destiny was. In other words, the Samaritans did not agree with that plan and purpose. When this happened, the disciples asked the Lord if they could call fire down out of heaven to destroy the Samaritans! After all, shouldn't the sinners be punished? The Lord told them they did not know what manner of spirit they were obeying. He came to save the lost, not destroy

them. These were the very disciples of Jesus and
they were listening to the wrong spirit. What spirit
are you listening to? Is it the spirit of love or
another kind of spirit? Only the spirit of love will
take you down the pathway of righteousness.

Are you throwing stones because of
somebody's sin? Are you condemning someone
because they disobey the Word of God? How do you
treat your children when they fail to live up to your
expectations? What groups of people do you want to
see punished and condemned for their sin? In Luke
6:35-36 the Lord tells us to be merciful as our Father
in heaven is merciful. He is kind to the evil and to
those who are not thankful. We are to be kind to
them as well. Jesus told the Pharisees that although
they paid tithes and kept some of the word, they
forgot the weightier matters of the word - justice,
mercy, and honor. He said in John 6:54 that we
cannot get into heaven unless we eat the flesh and
drink the blood of the Son of God. Many people left
Jesus that day and did not follow him because they
thought he meant it literally. To eat the flesh and
drink the blood of the Lord Jesus Christ means to
eat his Word or to live by his Word. In John chapter
1, it lets us know that Jesus is the Word of God.
Verse 14 tells us that this Word, or Jesus, became
flesh. When He said to eat his flesh, he meant to eat
Him who is the Word of God. The Lord told us in
Matthew 4:4 that man does not live just by bread,

but by the Word of God. To eat God's Word, which is the flesh of Jesus, is to live by His words.

I once heard a man say that he wished he had a machine gun so he could gun down all of the heretics that were against him. This man claimed to be a Christian! Prejudice and lack of forgiveness have led so many down the wrong road. The Lord said the way to heaven was narrow and difficult (Matthew 7:14). He said few people are on this road. He also said that many were on the broad road that leads to destruction. That road has anything you want on it and you can do whatever you want on that road. You can even be very self-righteous and still be on the broad road that leads to eternal damnation. The Lord said the straight and narrow road leads to eternal life. That is the road that is tight and narrow. It is a very hard road because it requires you to die to yourself and your ways and follow the ways of Jesus in everything. It requires you to love your enemies. It requires you to walk in mercy and forgiveness.

In 1 John 4:7-8 we are told to love one another because that is what it means to be born of God. Why is it important to be born of God? The Lord said unless you are born again you cannot enter into the kingdom of heaven. God is Love, so you must be born of Love. Those who do not walk in love continually do not know God because God is love. To walk in love continually means you are sold out to love and you are eagerly pursuing this love. According to Paul in 1 Corinthians 14:1, we should pursue love. It should be our great quest and aim in life. Obviously, we are humans and we will make mistakes and fail to walk in love on occasion. But walking in love should become our way of life, and we should repent and ask the Lord's forgiveness immediately when we fail to love. Love is your new treasure, which is where your heart should be. To be born of God means to love God and it means to know him. You cannot know him unless you are born of love and you cannot have eternal life unless you know him. Therefore, you must be first born of love, then you can know him, and only then can you have eternal life. The Lord Jesus said in John 17:3 that the way to have Eternal Life is to know the only true God and Jesus Christ whom he sent to earth.

The Word tells us the very first and greatest commandment is to love the Lord our God with all our heart, soul, mind, and body. The second greatest commandment is to love our neighbor as ourselves. So many are trying to live the Great Commission without doing the Great Commandment! That is why the Lord said that many will come to him in that day and say 'Lord, Lord,' and will not enter into the kingdom of God. Why not? They did not do the will of God. He called them workers of iniquity and told them to depart. He said he did not KNOW them. God is love. If we walk in love, we know God; if we do not walk in love, we do not know God. This love should become our very nature and we are to grow in it and seek it every day.

In 2 Peter 1:4 we are told that God has given us exceedingly great and precious promises of his Word so we can partake of his divine nature. His promises are yes and amen through Jesus Christ our Lord. Peter said we are born again, not of corruptible seed but of incorruptible seed, by the Word of God. This word is like seed and contains the very nature of God. When we are born of the Word, the nature of God comes inside of us. 2 Corinthians 5:17-18 says it another way – "if anyone is in Christ, he is a new creation; old things have passed away" and all things are new. Notice it did not say all things are new except generational curses. Once we have been born again, old things are passed away. Wake up, Christians! Old things are passed away! Why do so many Christians continue to raise the old man and partake of his nature when we have been born again and can partake of the new nature of Jesus Christ? Why would anybody want to resurrect a generational curse when it is passed away with the spiritual re-birth? One reason is that the sin is still loved. It is comfortable and familiar. Take off that old nature and partake of the new divine nature!

The story of Lot's wife should be a warning to all who live for Christ. She was a believer. When it came time to leave their familiar surroundings and to do what God had called them to do, she disobeyed God's Word by looking back, and she became a pillar of salt. Why did she look back? She loved that world and its ways more than she loved God's Word and his ways. The Word says that sin brings pleasure for a season. To resist that sin is a fight of the spirit and the flesh. You have to realize, though, that you have been given dominion over sin. Do not give up the fight of learning to crucify your flesh and keeping the body of sin under control. It is a choice you make from within your heart. What path will you follow? Will it be the pathway of love? If you have been making the wrong choices, now is your chance to repent immediately and follow after Christ. He has forgiveness ready and waiting for you. 1 John 1:9 tells us that if we confess our sin, he will forgive us and cleanse us from all our unrighteousness.

In Revelation 3:15-16 the Lord told the lukewarm church to repent of being lukewarm or he would spew them out of his mouth. Notice he wrote that to the church, not the world. He went on to tell them that he was knocking at their heart and if any would open the door and let him in, then he and the Father would come in and sup with them. I thought he was already in the heart of the church! He came into their hearts at the time of salvation, so they must have not kept him there. What did they do to remove him from their hearts? If you notice in the parable of the sower in Mark 4, the Word of God (Jesus) was sown into the hearts of people who became believers. This Word (Jesus) can be taken out of the heart of the believer as well. Sometimes Satan comes in and immediately steals it. At other times, persecution or cares of this world or deceitfulness of riches can choke Him out of you. In other words, He will no longer be living in you. Only those who produce fruit in their lives have Jesus the Word living in them. Was the lukewarm church in that condition because they were not walking in love? Were they not walking in love because love was no longer in them? In Revelation 2:4-5, in the first letter to the churches, he told them to repent because they had left their first love. Today's salvation message has made it sound so easy for people to be a part of the kingdom of God. The word "repent" is being left out of many altar calls. The part that commands us to turn away from sin and follow the living God is being left out of the message. He commands us to walk in love.

In 1 Corinthians 13:4-8 the Holy Spirit inspired the Apostle Paul and gave him the definition of love. Read it in the Amplified version of the Bible and begin to let the Holy Spirit deal with you. Do you take account of the evil done to you by

others? Do you insist on your own rights or your
own way? Do you believe the best of every person?
Meditate on those words and ask yourself, "Is that
me?" If not, then repent and ask the Lord to forgive
you. Turn your life toward following his way of love.
He is right there standing at your heart's door,
knocking and waiting for you to open it up to him.
Turn to love; it is the most excellent way.

In Matthew 24:12 the Lord Jesus said that
iniquity will abound in the last days and that the
love of many will become cold or hardened. The love
he refers to is the God kind of love that can only be
found in Christians. These are the last days and we
are seeing just that. Remember that iniquity means
lawlessness, which means doing less than what the
law requires. God's Word tells us in James 2:8 to
fulfill the royal law, which is to love your neighbor as
yourself. As Christians, the law we are to live by is
the law of love. If we do anything less than what
this law requires, we are walking in iniquity. The
abundance of iniquity is what will make love become
hardened like cold wax. Many people will be living
and doing less than what Love tells them to do.
Remember, the greatest commandment is to love the
Lord your God with all of your heart, soul, mind, and
body. To walk in that love requires that you be so in
love with God that you make every effort to walk in
his ways according to his word and his truth, and to
turn away from everything that tries to hinder you.

In 1 Corinthians 13:5 we are told that this love keeps no record of any evil or wrong done to it. If you don't forgive those who hurt you, then you are taking account of the evil done to you. Love and forgiveness are requirements for eternal life and heaven. In Romans 13:10 it tells us that love does no harm to its neighbor. Earlier, in verse 8, we are told to owe no man anything except to love him. Love is required every day. If we do anything less than what the law of love requires, we are walking in iniquity. Do you remember what the Lord said in Mathew 7:23? He told the workers of iniquity to depart from him because he never knew them. In 1 John 3:15 the Word says that if we hate our brother, we are a murderer and we do not have eternal life abiding in us. He wrote this to Christians! Yes, Christians can hate their fellow brothers and sisters. We tend to think of the word "hate" as being very harsh and extreme. However, in the original Greek, it actually means to simply love less – to love less than what is required.

You can do all kinds of good deeds and help many people, but if you have ill will toward them, you are not walking in love. In 1 Corinthians 13:3 it says that even if I give away all I own to help the poor and allow my body to be burned, there is no profit for me unless I have love. The Lord said in Mathew 6:14-15 that if you forgive men of their trespasses then your Father in heaven will forgive you of your trespasses, but if you don't forgive men their trespasses then your Father in heaven will not forgive you of your trespasses. If you need to forgive someone, now is the time to ask the Lord to forgive you. Then go and ask the one you have not forgiven to forgive you as well. It is important that you do it as quickly as possible. If that someone has died, then you can talk to the Lord and let him know what you would do if they were alive. Do not be deceived into thinking that you can do enough good things to offset this lack of forgiveness. You must be obedient to his Word and his ways. Forgiveness is one of them.

As my son was walking home from school one day, he and his best friend had a fight. Since he was larger than his friend, the smaller boy went home crying. My son then went to another friend's house to play. While he was playing in the front yard with this other friend, the parents of the first boy came into the yard and began to yell at him for what he had done. Because of the noise, several neighbors came out into their yards to see what was happening. It actually became so intense that the older sister of my son's second friend considered calling 911 for help. You can probably imagine how I felt to discover that a 6-foot 250-pound man and his wife were screaming threats at my 12-year-old son.

When I came home from work and heard the story from my son, I made a phone call to the parents to find out from them what had happened. They felt they had the right to yell at him because of his actions to their son. There was no repentance or regret. In fact, I was yelled at in much the same way as he had been. I was upset not only because of my son's verbal abuse, but also because these were Christian neighbors – they were believers in Jesus Christ! It was fortunate that I didn't get to speak much - I wanted to quote the Bible to them and it would have been the wrong time and with the wrong attitude! I prayed and prayed about this. I finally began to practice what love would do. I began to pray for them. In Mathew 5:44 we are told to "love your enemies,... and pray for those who spitefully use you and persecute you." It also tells us to "do good to those who hate you" (love you less than they should). So, when Christmas arrived, I sent these parents a letter asking them to forgive me of any ill will I may have caused. I included a gift certificate to a nice restaurant. The father became very apologetic and we made peace. Love is the most excellent way.

According to the Word of God, love is not a choice but a command. In John 13:34-35 the Lord said, "A new commandment I give to you, that you love one another; as I have loved you, that you also love one another. By this all will know that you are

My disciples, if you have love for one another."
Notice that you do not get the choice of whom you
will love and whom you will not. We are commanded
to love one another the same way the Lord has loved
us. How did he love us? He gave himself totally and
completely for us. We are to give ourselves to one
another. The choice we have is whether we want to
obey his words. If you are not practicing loving one
another, then you are practicing sin. 1 Corinthians
13:8 tells us that love never fails. This does not
necessarily mean that the person you are showing
love toward will change. It means you will not fail
before the Lord because you have chosen to obey
Him by walking in love.

In today's society, we can buy something from
somebody on credit. That means we then have to
make regular payments to them until the cost of the
item has been paid. If we do not make the payment,
we are defaulting on our agreement with them. If
we continue to miss payments, they can prosecute us
and put us in jail. In Romans 13:8 the Word of God
tells us to "owe no one anything except to love one
another." We are told to make the payment of love
to those around us every day. We have no choice in
the matter if we are Christians. We have to love one
another because that is what we are commanded to
do. If we are born again, according to Paul in 1
Corinthians 14:1, our greatest pursuit or aim in life
should be to love one another. That is what we

should be living for – not simply for ourselves. If we do not make this payment each day, then we default on our agreement with the Lord as Christians. We can be taken captive by Satan if we do not acknowledge the truth or act on that knowledge (2 Timothy 2:24-26). Paul told Timothy that many Christians find themselves in this position. The devil has snared them because he has deceived them into not walking in love. They are actually opposing themselves because they should be walking in love, but they have chosen to disobey by listening to Satan and not walking in love to one another. If they want to escape from the snare, they must ask God for repentance (verse 25) and start acting on the knowledge of the truth. The truth is that we are to walk in love every day and we owe this to every man. Love is the most excellent way and it is the WAY to follow.

If we do the will of God that the Lord Jesus spoke of in Matthew 7, then we will have eternal life. Walking in the God kind of love is his will. In 1 Timothy chapter 2 the Word of God tells us that God's will is that he wants all men to be saved and to come to the knowledge of the truth. He wants all men to know the truth. In John 14 the Lord Jesus said he was the way, the TRUTH, and the life. If the will of God is for us to know the truth and the Lord Jesus is the truth, then he wants all men to know Jesus. In John 17 the Lord said that eternal life was

to know God and Jesus Christ whom he sent. The
Word of God tells us that God is love (1 John 4:8). If
eternal life is to know God, then eternal life is to
know love since God is love. Do you see where we
have missed it in most of our preaching? Love is the
greatest way and should be preached and taught
from the time we are born. I am talking about the
God kind of love and not man's kind of love. This is
God's way and not man's way. This God kind of love
is the key to everything.

PREPARE THE WAY

When the Lord Jesus Christ was here on the earth, he had a simple message. It was simply to "Repent, for the kingdom of heaven is at hand" (Mathew 4:17). John the Baptist had a message to prepare the way of the Lord. His message in Mathew 3:2 was also to "Repent, for the kingdom of heaven is at hand!" The message has not changed, yet it has been sugar-coated today to keep it from being "offensive". Yes, you can come as you are and accept Jesus into your heart. Yes, he will forgive you of your sins and make you whole. But something very important is missing today – repentance. You must turn away from the sin in your life and follow Jesus.

God commands "all men everywhere to repent" (Acts 17:30). We are to run away from our sin and walk in truth. The Lord had to deal with the early church as well as the church today regarding repentance. The Apostle Paul had to deal with sin in the church as well (I Corinthians 5). Evidently it was being reported that fornication was occurring in the church. That means people were having sexual intercourse without being married. Even worse, someone had fornicated with his step-mother! The Apostle Paul was livid that the fellow believers did nothing about it. It sounds so much like the church today. He went on to tell the church that he is delivering that individual to Satan for the destruction of the flesh so that his spirit MAY be saved in the day of the Lord Jesus. Do you mean that this person, who was a believer in Jesus Christ, was being turned over to Satan in hopes that in the day of the Lord he MAY be saved? You see how the church today has changed? We do nothing about sin in the church. Paul encouraged them to put that wicked person away.

In the second letter he wrote to the church, he again dealt with someone within the church who had sinned. He said in 2 Corinthians 2:4 that he wrote the first letter not to grieve the church over these matters, but that they would know the love he had toward them. They had dealt with the person who had sinned and that person had grieved over his sin. He had repented and turned away from it. Paul continued (7:8-10) that although he had made them sorry by his previous letter, he saw that it had led them to repentance. He said that "godly sorrow produces repentance leading to salvation,... but the sorrow of the world produces death." So many people are told to not worry about their sin because God understands that we live in a carnal body and he knows we are weak. They are told not to worry because he will forgive them. There is rarely any mention of being sorry and turning away from their sinful ways.

David, God's anointed one, committed adultery and murder. When he was confronted by the prophet of God, he repented of his sin and prayed to God because he had sinned against God and against heaven. Many people ask God to forgive them because they got caught, not because they are sorry for their sin. They try to have accountability before men when they should have it before God. He is the one you are sinning against and hurting. He is the one you must stand before on the Day of Judgment. He is the one who will forgive us of our sins and cleanse us from all unrighteousness (1 John 1:9). So many Christians today believe that it is "normal" for them to still be sinning every day. Sin is actually expected within many churches! I wonder where they get that kind of thinking. Does it become okay to sin every day just because everyone else does it? In 1 John 3:8 we are told that he who practices sin is of the devil, but in verse 9 it says that whoever is born of God does not practice sin.

It is time for the church to repent and prepare the way of the Lord and to make straight his paths. In the letters written to the churches in the book of Revelation, the Lord tells the churches at least seven times to repent! Notice that these letters are written to the churches - believers in Jesus Christ. The Lord is instructing the Christians to repent before he comes.   If they do not, they must face the consequence. Yes, he continually offers forgiveness and grace, but only as we repent of our sins.

We live in a feel-good society, which fulfills the Apostle Paul's prophecy in 2 Timothy 4:3 of church members going after teachers who will scratch their ears and tell them what they want to hear. These people don't want to hear what the Lord says.   They only want to hear about blessings, prosperity, health, and happiness. They don't want to hear the whole gospel.

In 1 John 2:1 it says these things were written for us so that we could avoid sin. Evidently we can live a life without sin. If we could not, then John would not have told the church to not sin.   He continued his letter (3:8-9) by saying that he who continually practices sin is of the devil. Whoever is born of God does not practice sin because he is born of God.   John then says that the way to tell the children of God from the children of the devil is that one practices sin and the other practices righteousness.

The Lord told a story about the wheat and the tares in Mathew 13:24-30. The enemy came and sowed tares in the middle of a wheat field. In other words, there are people who claim to be Christians but are not, yet they are in the midst of the true Christians in many churches all over the world. Some are false teachers, some false apostles, and some are disguised in sheep's clothing, yet inside they are ravening wolves. The Word tells us that some make merchandise of the true body of Christ and will take money from the true Christians (2 Peter 2:3). The Lord said in verse 30 to let them grow together (both the wheat and the tares) until the time of the harvest, then the tares will be burned and the wheat will go into God's barn. You cannot tell the difference yet between the wheat and the tares, and it will not be revealed until the Lord comes to take his harvest away.

Now you can see why the Lord said that many will come to him in that day and call him Lord, Lord but will not enter into the kingdom of heaven. These people profess to know God but in their actions they deny him (Titus 1:16). In Luke 13:23 someone came to the Lord Jesus and asked him if there were few that would be saved. He told them the only way to enter is at the strait gate. He told them that many will try to enter in other ways but will not be able. If you read on in this passage, he says that when the door is shut many will come to him and argue that they have eaten and drunk in his presence and have taught in his streets. The Lord will reply to them that he does not know them, and will tell them to depart from him. He will call them workers of iniquity. These are people who went to church and got saved once, but didn't think they had to go anymore or do what Jesus said to do in his Word. These are people who went to church and did what they believed was right, but not what the Lord told them to do. These are people who went to church and called themselves Christians.

If you are practicing any kind of sin, repent of it immediately and turn to the Lord Jesus Christ for forgiveness. He is right there when you do that. He will take you in and come into your heart and begin to fellowship with you. You must turn away from sin. It is time to turn away from those secretly visited pornographic web sites. It is time to turn away from fornication and adultery (sex that is forbidden by the Word of God). It is time to stop cheating on your taxes. It is time to turn away from hatred. Begin to hate the sin! Stop practicing it and turn to the Lord Jesus Christ. The time is now. Do not wait until tomorrow. Now is the time for salvation. Today is the day. Cry to the Lord with all your heart and tell Him you are repenting. Give him your whole heart. Follow him and him only. He loves you and is waiting with open arms for you to come to him.

In Mathew 25 the Lord tells the story of the ten virgins. They all had lamps, but five of the virgins were wise and five were foolish. The five wise virgins had oil in their lamps and the five foolish virgins did not. When the bridegroom came, they all awoke to meet him. Since the foolish virgins had no oil in their lamps, they could not light their lamps and go with the Lord. They asked the wise virgins to share some of their oil, but they were told to go buy their own oil for their lamps. However, it was too late. The bridegroom came and took the five wise virgins into the marriage and shut the door. These ten virgins represent Christians. Half of them were foolish. They were all waiting for their bridegroom, the Lord, yet only half of them were taken into heaven.

This is a parable and the percentages may not be as high as fifty percent, but evidently there are many people who think they are living a Christian life and are not. When the Lord returns, they will not have any oil in their lamps. I believe they are not walking in the love of God and are practicing iniquity instead. They are doing less than what the law of love requires.

In the letters written to the churches in Revelation there were many things mentioned that would befall the church if they did not repent. Three of these things stand out more than the others. The first thing mentioned was that they would be removed from their place with him. That church had left their first love. They were doing certain works, but the Lord still had something against them. This something could remove them from their place with him. The second thing mentioned was that he would vomit them out of his mouth. This was the lukewarm church. Their practice of being lukewarm made him vomit them out of his mouth. These are people who are Christians in the church of Jesus Christ, but have lost their zeal for him. The third thing mentioned was that their names would be blotted out of the Book of Life. Can you imagine going to church and doing what you believe is right, and then receiving a letter from the Lord telling you that your works are not perfect and if you do not repent he will blot your name out of the Book of Life? These were Christians whose works were not complete before God. These were Christians who said they had a name that they were alive but in reality they were dead. These people were saved. Their names had been entered into the Book of Life, but their names could be removed!

Paul wrote in Philippians to work out your own salvation with fear and trembling. I don't see much fear and trembling going on any more. I wonder why? The Word of God tells us in Ephesians 5:27 that the Lord is endeavoring to present the church spotless. That means without spot or blemish. We are told in 2 Peter 3:14 to "be diligent, to be found by Him in peace, without spot and blameless." The spotless Christians are keeping themselves pure for their bridegroom. They are following him and doing his will and not their own will.

The Lord loves his body and gave himself for it. If the body does not love the Lord with all of their heart, then it is in danger. He has sent his Word and his Spirit to guide us and keep us, but if we refuse and go our own way then we may miss heaven. We must forsake all and follow Him completely. Don't let pride convince you all is well when the Lord tries to show you something in need of repentance. Remember that pride goes before a fall.

God's Word tells us not to love the world or the things that are in the world (I John 2:15). All that is in the world is the lust of the flesh, the lust of the eyes, and the pride of life. In other words, it is the passion, the possessions, and the position that this world offers that keep the body from doing what it is called to do. If we love this world, we do not have the love of the Father. John wrote this to believers. It is an exhortation to believers in Christ to not love this world. That means the believer has a chance to fall out of love with God and in love with the world. If it were not possible then why would he write it to them? Paul said in 2 Timothy 4:10 that "Demas has forsaken me, having loved this present world." The world and its ways are what Satan uses to tempt us away from loving God and to loving the world instead.

The parable of the sower is a great message the Lord has given us to explain how Satan comes immediately to steal the Word of God out of our heart as soon as it is preached. Has Satan has been telling you anything as you have read these words? Has he suggested that what is being said is wrong because it does not line up with your denomination? Has he been trying to steal the Word right out of your heart? So many have been deceived in this hour - they stick to what their religious group believes rather than take a good look at the Word of God for themselves. They would rather listen to their denomination rather than the Word of God.

In Romans 12 Paul tells us to not be conformed to this world, but to be transformed by renewing our minds. The world loves to entertain us and to lure us away from being on fire for God. The world wants us to be consumed with possessions rather than to be generous with them. The world wants us to think we are something special when in reality we are supposed to be "dead" with Christ living inside of us. Do you give your passion to things of this world? Remember, the Lord says where your treasure is, that is where your heart is also. Is your heart going after the possessions or the passions or the positions of this world? When did Sunday night become a time of having Super Bowl parties in church instead of worshiping the living God who gives us all things?

Churches all over America are full, but how many truly love God? What is their reason for attending church? Do they go for themselves or for the Lord? Do they go to lift up Jesus and magnify him, or is it to be recognized? Is it to give or to receive? The church has settled for whatever the world has offered them. Where is the hunger to pursue the living God at the altars of our churches? Where are the prayers of God's children? Where are the sons and daughters of God that have separated themselves from the world and unto Him?

I was shocked during a visit to a large church when they announced their upcoming "American Idol" party. The television program would be viewed in the church! I thought we were not to worship idols? How deceived we have become! Have you noticed the change in the church? We have become entertainers in our preaching, our singing, and even in our announcements! We want the world to watch us and see how well we can do. We have cast our pearls before the swine. The church has become more of a Country Club than a place to worship and serve the Lord God Almighty. We bring the world in from the outside and conform to it rather than getting the world to conform to God.

The Lord is reaching out to you this very moment if you have not turned away from this world. It is soon to pass away and those who love it will pass away with it. Do not be deceived by those who tell you to simply follow your denomination or group. When you die, you will not stand before your denomination, but before the living God, and he will judge you according to his Word. Peter said that judgment begins at the house of God. The choice is yours - who will you serve? Will you repent and turn back to the Lord and follow the way of love?

The Apostle Paul tells us in Hebrews 12:1 to lay aside every weight and sin, and run the race with patience, looking unto Jesus. He is the author and developer of our faith. We were dead in our trespasses and sins, but he has made us alive (Ephesians 2:1). He made us alive with his life, so we can love him and one another. Eternal life is the very nature and life of God living inside of you. It is God himself now living in you. The Lord said to be separated from the world and touch not the world, then he will be our God and we will be his sons and daughters (2 Corinthians 6:17-18). It is time for the true sons and daughters of God to rise up and live the life God has come to give us. It is not fueled by possessions or positions of title or passions (of the flesh), but it is fueled by the life of God within. What excites you? What motivates you? Be honest with yourself - your eternity depends on it. Is it the

world and its things or is it the living God? What
motivates you when you wake up each day? Is it
something in this world or is it the Spirit of God
within you? Don't be fooled by this world and the
people in it. They will tell you that it's okay to need
something physical to pick you up and to get you
going. Nonsense! When you are alive with eternal
life, the life of God himself inside of you is all you
need to pick you up, get you going, and set you on
fire.

"But if the Spirit of Him who raised Jesus
from the dead dwells in you, He who raised Christ
from the dead will also give life to your mortal bodies
through His Spirit who dwells in you" (Romans
8:11). The living God is the one that lives inside of
his children. They do not need the things of this
world to excite them. They do not need a million
dollars or the chance to get a million dollars to
motivate them. The love of God within them
motivates them to love their enemies and to do good
to them who hate them and to bless them who curse
them and to pray for them who spitefully use them
and persecute them. They do not need a tax
incentive to make them give. They give because they
are motivated by the life of God inside of them. They
are not conformed to live the way the world lives, but
they are conformed to live according to the Word of
God. When they enter the sanctuary to praise the
Lord, they are ready to praise him. They do not need

the songs to pick them up and get them going - they are already on fire because of the life of God inside them.

I have witnessed a number of church splits, and it is amazing how the love of money was the root cause of most of them. The body has suffered immensely because the leaders of the church have become more motivated by money than by the life and love of God. Most church splits happen because of a lack of love. Paul said in 2 Timothy 3:5 that in the last days some people will love worldly pleasures more than God. He said they will have a form of Godliness (they will appear Godly), but they will deny its power. They will say they know God, but their actions and ways of living will not acknowledge knowing God (Titus 1:16). Remember, to know God is to love God. These people profess that they love God, yet they rob one another of money in church business and church splits. In Revelation 3:2 the Lord tells the church to be watchful and to strengthen the things that are ready to die, because their works are not complete before God. They have forgotten the life of God inside of them and they have let it die. Each new church group thinks it will be different from the group they just left. They build another church with stolen money and they think all is well. Where is the repentance? Where is the life and love of God?

Reconcile the differences you have had with others. Forgive those who have offended you and if you have robbed anyone in the name of God, then return it and reconcile with them. It is not worth missing heaven over. It is time to repent and to turn away from this world and its ways. It is time to turn away from your sins and to begin to call upon the living God. God Almighty told us that he will hear his people, forgive them, and heal them IF they humble themselves, pray to him, and turn away from their wicked ways (2 Chronicles 7:14). The Apostle Paul exhorts the church in 2 Corinthians 7:1 to "cleanse ourselves from all filthiness of the flesh and spirit." We are cleaned of all filthiness of the flesh and the spirit by the Word of God spoken to us (John 15:2-3). The Lord has spoken His Word to the body to cleanse it, so He may present it to God without spot or wrinkle (Ephesians 5:26-27). He is endeavoring to get his church ready and it must be clean. Peter gives an exhortation to the body of Christ in 2 Peter 3 about the coming, or return, of the Lord. In verse 11 he basically tells us that in preparation for his return we should be living a godly life filled with holy conduct. In other words, the way we should live this life separated to the Lord Jesus and follow his godly ways. In verse 14 he tells us that knowing these things, we should be found when he returns in peace, without spot, and blameless. Are you preparing yourself for when he returns, knowing that the time may be short? Are you separated to him alone or are you following God and this world? Where is your heart? Is it in following the ways of God or are you being found with spots in your life? Do not listen to those who tell you not to worry because everyone has some spots in their life. You do not stand before those people when you die. You must stand before the Lord himself and give an account of everything you have done. It is time to repent. Turn from your sin and prepare the way of the Lord. The life of God is available to whosoever will and the time is now. This is the day of salvation.

THE GREAT GIFT

In John 10:10 the Lord Jesus said, "I have come that they may have life, and that they may have it more abundantly." The purpose for his coming was to give us eternal life. He came to get us to know him. Remember that life eternal, according to John 17:3, is to know the only true God, and Jesus Christ.

Paul said to taste and see that the Lord is good. When you taste the Lord and the life he has come to give, you will want nothing else in this life. It is the most satisfying experience on the face of this earth. Nothing has or ever will compare to having eternal life. And then to have it in abundance is even more amazing! When I was younger, I had many experiences with what this world has to offer. None of it cannot compare to knowing God. His life keeps on living and loving when everything around you is falling apart. His life excites you every moment of every day. His life loves and keeps on loving in the middle of a crooked and perverse society. It is beautiful and wonderful to have it and to live it. It keeps you loving when going to work may seem like a pain. It lets you constantly see the best of every person no matter how evil they may seem or whatever things they may have done.

John tells us in I John 5:11-12 that "God has given us eternal life and this life is in His Son. He who has the Son has life, he who does not have the Son of God does not have life." The word life in the original writing is the Greek word ZOE which means the God kind of life. God's own life is given to you when you receive eternal life. You actually receive God himself inside of you! God never forces himself into anyone and will not stay unless He is welcomed. He does not take you over unless you invite him to. He wants to show everyone what he has given them and what he has waiting for them. The Word says that if any man is in Christ Jesus, he is a new creation - old things are passed away and all things are new (2 Corinthians 5:17-18). All things are now of God, who brought us back into friendship with himself by the work that Jesus Christ did for us at his cross. Old things, your old life, are passed away. Generational curses are passed away. All of your sins are passed away. Everything in you that was old is now gone, and all things have now become new.

When I was 20 years old, my life was full of misery. I felt like no one loved me and life had no meaning. I searched high and low for all the things this world had to offer and nothing satisfied. Drugs, sex, sports, religion, you name it, none of it satisfied. It only left me with an empty feeling. It brought pleasure to my flesh for a time, but it still left me feeling empty inside. Along with it came anxiety, loneliness, guilt, depression, and rejection. I finally got to the point that I did not want to live. What was there to live for? No one truly loved me, it seemed. I was rejected on all sides. The pain and agony I felt every night at bedtime was not something I wanted to live with the rest of my life. I had gone to church all of my life and there was no life there. Everyone that went there seemed to have the same feelings and problems I did, to one degree or another. Most were trying to fill that void inside with whatever this world has to offer. We try so hard to make ourselves feel good and take way the pain that we will do almost anything to get away from all of the emotions tied up within us. We put on a good show on the outside, but the inside is dead or about to die.

One New Year's Eve night, I was walking down the back alley of an apartment complex near where I grew up. I looked up to the sky and asked God, if he was really there, to send me a friend. Send someone that will love me and be with me. Send someone I can talk with. A few months later, I thought my prayer was answered. I met a girl who became my friend and we eventually started dating. About a year or so later, while we were still dating, she began to cheat on me and flirt with other guys. All of those old feelings of rejection surfaced again, and the loneliness was even worse this time. We continued to date, however. One day when I picked her up from the church she attended, she was crying as she got into the car. I noticed there was something different about her. She tried to explain the change that had taken place in her heart, but I did not understand. She invited me to come to church with her, but because of prejudice in my upbringing, I thought it would be wrong to enter that church. A few months later, my dad died and I felt the only friend I ever had in life was gone. Now I felt truly alone.

One Sunday night, I finally decided to visit the church with my girl friend. It was a very small church. Maybe about 10 or 15 people were there, and they were very friendly. I felt a love coming from those people that I had never experienced in church before. I don't remember much of what the Pastor preached from the Word of God except for one point. He said that if we would open our hearts, repent, and accept Jesus Christ, then he would become our BEST Friend. My heart leaped and I remembered that New Year's Eve night when I had asked God to send me a friend. When the Pastor gave the invitation, I went to the altar. When I knelt down, I started to cry because I realized I was a sinner and I was very repentant of what I had done in my life. I no longer wanted to live that life and I wanted to turn away from it. I cried for what seemed like hours, and then all of a sudden I felt something happen inside of me. All of that pain, all of that rejection, all of that guilt, depression, and loneliness suddenly left me. It was like someone or something had lifted a two-ton weight off of my chest. I felt light as a feather and so free. Then something even more wonderful happened. The love of God was poured into my heart by the Holy Spirit of God. For the first time in my life, I felt love in its purest form. I felt His joy and His peace. I became a brand new creation because of Jesus Christ. Eternal life entered into me and it has been there ever since.

God has given us all things freely. Why would you want what this world offers when he alone can give you life abundantly? Wherever you are or whatever you are doing, you must recognize that you have sinned and that the void in your heart cannot be filled with earthly things. They are only temporary and will pass away. You cannot get abundant life by doing good things. This life God has given us is eternal and will never pass away, but it only comes through Jesus Christ. If you will repent of your sinful ways and begin to call upon the Lord, he will come inside of you and become your best Friend. He will bring his eternal life inside of you. Let him make something beautiful of your life. He loves you.

My wife and I visited a number of churches in our area. We met a lot of nice people. We saw nice buildings with beautiful music, comfortable seating, donuts, coffee, bagels, meeting rooms for first time visitors, and all kinds of programs to get the entire family involved. Everything looked so wonderful. As we visited these places, though, we began to notice something - the musicians and worship leaders sang praises to God, but the majority of the people in the crowd did not join in. They just watched the others sing and then when it was all over they clapped their hands for them. This was carried out in almost every service and in every place of worship. There were a few that raised their hands every now and then, and a few did sing, but the majority did nothing but watch. Most of these church services looked like a concert.

One placed we visited had a very interesting message, teaching that church members should get involved with helping others. The Pastor told of an event that he and another family had experienced. While eating at a restaurant, they saw someone put a flier in the window. The flier said that there was a search for a missing 5-year-old girl. After their meal, the Pastor and this family went by to visit the family whose daughter was missing. The neighborhood was active with people getting together to search for this little girl. The police were searching with helicopters and there were search parties combing the area. Why were all these people involved in helping with the search? The Pastor

pointed out that it was because it became personal to
them. Maybe they had children or grandchildren
close to this little girl's age. Unfortunately, the little
girl was found dead. The family then contacted the
Pastor to do the funeral. They were thankful to him.
He was the only Pastor in the area that had visited
them and had gotten involved. This family did not
have a church home and they wanted him to do the
funeral. They then began to come to his church.
Why? He had taken their need personally and had
gotten involved.

There is another point to this story, though.
Is God even personal to us? When it comes time to
worship God, do we make our worship personal or do
we just sit there like bumps on a log? Is the Lord
personal to you during a worship service? Before we
can get personal with showing Christ's love to
others, we must get personal with the One we are
representing. Many Christians come to church
simply to ease their conscience or for a social event.
They say they know God but they do not show it in
their actions (Titus 1:16). When you know God, you
want to praise and worship him with all of your
heart, soul, mind, and body. If shouting or singing
in a church service makes you feel uncomfortable,
you will not like heaven! It's all about worship, and
there will be plenty of singing and shouting and
praising God. The Word of God tells us (all of us) to
shout and sing praises to our Lord and King. That

means the whole congregation and not just the
singers up front. It also says to do it with your
whole heart.

I know there are times of silence while
worshiping quietly with tears, but there are also
times of praising him with all kinds of joyful noise.
The reason many do not praise him is because they
do not know him. They do not understand the great
and mighty things he has done for them. They have
never experienced this great love from above.
Worship applies to more than just church services,
too. We are to worship him in our everyday lives as
well. Do you worship him in your actions by obeying
his Word? Do you talk about him? Do you praise
him all the day long? Is he your passion from the
time you wake up until the time you go to sleep?

In Luke 7:36-50 the Lord visited the house of
a Pharisee named Simon. A woman came to Jesus
while he was there. She began to cry, washing his
feet with her tears. She then dried his feet with her
hair, kissed his feet, and anointed them with
fragrant oil. When the Pharisee saw it, he began to
have doubts about Jesus being a prophet. Surely
Jesus would have known that this woman was a
sinner if he were a prophet. Simon questioned
whether Jesus knew this woman. The Lord then
asked Simon some questions about a creditor who
had two debtors. If one owed him 500 pence and the

other owed him 50 pence, and both were forgiven of their debts, which one would love their creditor the most? Simon answered correctly that the one who he forgave the most would love him the most. The Lord knows those that love him, because they worship him with everything they have. They show it in their works, or actions. This woman displayed her knowledge of God, because she knew what he had done for her. He was personal to her and she showed it to him in her actions.

The Father wants us to worship him in Spirit and in Truth (John 4:23-24). God is a Spirit and they that worship him MUST worship him in Spirit and in Truth. That means we must worship him with our heart and with our actions. We cannot limit our worship to just what makes us feel comfortable, but we must worship in whatever way pleases the Lord. I know that shouting and singing alone does not indicate true worship. People can sing and shout in church, but deny him in their actions during the rest of the week. The principle is similar to the acts of loving and giving. The Word tells us that you can give without loving (1 Corinthians 13:1-3) but you can't show love without giving (1 John 3:16-17). That is why love is the key to everything. True worship is actually a way of life that is performed every day and everywhere, but it becomes evident in the sanctuary when it comes time to bless the Name of the Lord. Is he personal to you? Do not deceive yourself. Be honest with yourself and ask yourself if you really love God with all of your heart, soul, mind, and body. Your actions will show what is in your heart. The Lord said in Matthew 15:7-9 that people will worship Him with their lips but their hearts will be far from Him.

The Lord Jesus said that if we love him we will keep his commandments. The way we are sure that we know God is if we keep his commandments (1 John 2:3-6). Whoever says that they know God and does not keep his commands is a liar and the truth is not in him. People have been taught so much the doctrines or teachings of man and not the truth of God's Word. What does the Word say about praise and worship? Read it very carefully and ask yourself how it applies to you. Are you showing God you love him by keeping his commands? Are you listening to the commandments of God or those of men?

When I was only a year old in the Lord, I read what his Word says about lifting our hands to the Lord. I can remember the very first time I decided to lift my hands to praise God during a worship service. I felt like everybody in the church was looking at me! The Word also says that we are to shout to the Lord. We should do these things from our heart in order to please Him. Shouting or lifting your hands to Him certainly does not make you a Christian, but being a

Christian should make you want to please the Lord and do what he says. We are told in 1 John 2:5 that the love of God is perfected (matured) in whoever keeps his Word. That is how we know we are in him. That is how we know him. This applies in every area of our lives. When we know the Lord, we will walk in his ways and do his works.

Luke 6:27-36 tells us to love our enemies and to be kind to the evil and to those that are not thankful. Are you worshiping the Lord by doing just that? Do you show love to those who hate you? Are you kind to the evil? Do not let yourself be deceived. Paul said in Galatians 6:7 that we will reap whatever we sow in life. Your words and the actions that you do every day are a very important part of your worship.

To those that know him, the love of God is maturing and being perfected in them. Is he personal to you? Are you serious when you come into his presence to praise him and worship him, or are you there just to watch and be entertained? I suggest you pray like the Apostle Paul did with the Philippian church in Philippians 3:8. He said that he counted everything he had ever achieved in life as dung, and his desire was to know Jesus and the power of His resurrection and the fellowship of His sufferings, being made conformable to His death. Eternal life, according to the Lord in John 17:3, is

knowing God, the only true God, and Jesus Christ
whom he sent. James said to draw near to God and
he will draw near to you. Now is the time. Now is
the day of salvation.

If you need to repent of laziness or lack of
passion or commitment, then do so now. Commit to
trust God with everything you are. Begin to love
him and keep his Words. Talk with him every day
and get to know him more. As you draw near to him,
he draws near to you. Think about that. If you are
far away from an object, you get only a fuzzy idea of
what it is you are looking at. As you draw closer,
though, the object becomes clearer and clearer. You
begin to see all of the details and the beauty of
whatever it is you are nearing. The same is true
with the Lord. As you draw closer to him with your
heart and your actions, you begin to see how
beautiful he is. You see how compassionate and
loving he is and how he cares so much for you. You
see how good he is and how he desires to talk with
you and be with you. You cannot know him
intimately from a distance, but only as you draw
closer to him.

The children of Israel had the opportunity to
draw near to God in Exodus 19:10-11. The Lord told
Moses to tell the people to prepare themselves to
meet God. They were told to sanctify themselves for
two days, and on the third day God would come

down to visit them. In verse 16, the Lord came down. We do not get the reaction of the people until chapter 20 verses 18-21. The people were afraid and did not want to see God, but instead they wanted Moses to talk to God for them. They did not want to draw near to God. They wanted someone else to do it for them. In verse 21, Moses drew near but the people stood afar off. This is a type and shadow of this generation.

When the Lord Jesus was resurrected and ascended up to heaven, he said he would return. That was almost 2,000 years ago. The Word of God tells us that a thousand years is as a day to the Lord. It has been almost 2,000 years which equates to two days - the same amount of time the children of Israel were given to prepare to meet God. We are nearing the end of the 2,000 years and we are all going to meet God. The children of Israel were told to sanctify themselves and wash their clothes. They had to set themselves apart and get clean. The Word of God tells us to be holy, without spot or blemish on our garments. It tells us to separate ourselves from this world and its ways and its actions and the things it indulges itself with. We cannot get comfortable with this world - we should be preparing to meet the King! We should be cleaning our garments by washing them with the water of God's Word and doing what his Words are telling us. We should be preparing ourselves to draw near to God.

Most people today do not take the time to
draw near to God. They are too busy with the
pursuit of this world and its things. They want the
Pastor to draw near to God and tell them what God
is saying. They want him to go to God on their
behalf. It is primarily because they are not prepared
to meet God. They are indulging in things they
should not, and they do not even know him. That is
why they are afraid to meet him. Their garments
have spots and blemishes, and they are not readying
themselves to draw near to God. They are not laying
aside weights and sins. They are not living the life
God has given them to live. That is why many will
call to him "Lord, Lord" after the door has been shut.
They will tell him they were in his presence and
taught by him, but he will tell them he does not
know them. They were not walking in his love.
They were not preparing the way for the Lord's
return.

In Revelation 3:1-5 the Lord tells his church,
the believers in Jesus, that although they claim to
have a name that they are alive, they are really
dead. You see so many churches with wonderful
names on them declaring life, but many of them are
dead. He told the church to be watchful and to
strengthen the things that are ready to die. He told
them their works were not perfect or complete before
God. He said they should repent and remember how
they first received him and heard of him, and to hold

fast to those things. He said their garments were defiled and not white. The Lord Jesus told them that if they did not overcome these things, he would blot their name out of the Book of Life. He wrote this to his followers! You mean they can have their names blotted out of the Book of Life? The Lord said unless they repent, that is exactly what would happen.

I have some news for you. The Word of God does not support the coming of the great revival that has been prophesied for years by many preachers. Some people have a tendency to prophesy out of their flesh or by what they see rather than hearing from the living God. They tell you great things are about to happen to you and your family. They tell you God is about to do a mighty work. They call it the end time revival. But the Word of God has painted such a different picture.

Yes, people are still going to get saved and filled with the Holy Spirit. Yes, the gifts of the Spirit are still going to be in operation in these last days. But the Spirit of God speaks very emphatically in 1 Timothy 4:1 that in the last days "some will depart from the faith, giving heed to deceiving spirits and doctrines of demons." It says you can depart from the faith! Even though you have the faith, you can leave it! You have to have the faith before you can depart from it. In 2 Timothy

3:1-7 the Word clearly points out that the last days will be perilous times, which actually means they will be hard to deal with and difficult to bear. It goes on to describe the very generation we live in. He said they will have a form of Godliness but deny the power that comes from God. It goes on to say that deceivers will grow worse and worse, deceiving and being deceived.

Before the Lord actually returns to take the church away, which we call the rapture, two things must occur (2 Thessalonians 2:1-3). One is that the man of sin, the Antichrist, will be revealed. He will be revealed before the church is actually raptured! The church will not get raptured before he is revealed. The other thing mentioned, and listen very carefully to what it says, is that there shall be a falling away first before the man of sin is revealed. Where does an end-time revival fit into this picture? It clearly states that there is going to be a falling away. The word actually used in the Greek is an apostasy, which means a defecting from the truth. Understand this - you have to know the truth before you can defect from it. The only way to know the truth, according to the Lord in John 8, is to believe on Jesus and continue in his Words. According to the Apostle Paul then, people will be defecting from the truth in Christianity rather than living it. It did not say they would stop going to church, but they will defect from the truth of God's Word. We are seeing that happen before our very eyes.

You can understand now why the Lord said that many will call Him "Lord, Lord" and yet will still miss out on eternal life. The Lord himself stated in Matthew 24:12 that in the last days, iniquity will abound and the love of many will become cold. That love he speaks of is agape, which is the God kind of love. The iniquity or lawlessness of many people will come against every individual on this earth, and the Lord said that many of those who possess this agape will grow cold. They will not operate in this love, but will instead operate in the opposite of love, which is iniquity. Those who practice iniquity will not enter in, but will be told to depart (Matthew 7:23). Do not be amazed at the sin and iniquities that continue to grow. It was prophesied that this generation will be lovers of self and lovers of pleasure rather than lovers of God. We are seeing it increase before our very eyes as we watch God's Word come to pass.

Hebrews 2:1-3 tells us that we should listen very intently to the things God has spoken to us about eternal life. The question is, how are we going to escape punishment if we neglect the salvation God has given us? We are not to neglect this Great Gift God has given us. Wherever you are, if you are not ready and have not cleaned your garments, then you will miss God. The Lord says in Revelation 3 that if we are in that condition, we should counsel with him to buy gold tried in the fire and get white clothes so we are not naked before him. He says in verse 19 to be full of zeal and repent. In other words, get on fire for him and turn away from the way you are living. Now is the time. Your eternity depends on it.

FAITH WITHOUT WORKS IS DEAD

Paul wrote to the church of Ephesus to remind them of how they used to live and how the great love and mercy of God came to them to deliver them and save them (Ephesians 2:1-9). He told them that it is by grace we are saved through faith. It is not anything we can do ourselves. Our works cannot save us, so we cannot boast. Salvation is a gift of God. Paul was explaining that there is no way that your salvation can come to you except through the gift that God has given you, and you acquired it through faith. In Titus 2:11 we are told that the grace of God brings salvation. We cannot do anything to get this salvation except by God's grace bringing it to us, and we receive it by faith.

Paul wrote to the church at Rome to let them know that "Abraham believed God, and it was accounted to him for righteousness" (Romans 4:3). In other words, the only way Abraham could be righteous before God was to believe what God said to him. It was not any works that Abraham did that justified him before God, but it was God's grace and Abraham's belief. Paul also quoted David in Romans 4:8 when he wrote, 'Blessed is the man to whom the LORD shall not impute sin." It simply states that Abraham was not justified by works but by grace through faith. It sounds very similar to what Paul told the church at Ephesus. It sounds very similar to what we hear being preached... almost.

What was Paul saying in the scriptures? He was saying that our works before salvation do not count toward our righteousness. The Word of God informs us that man's righteousness, or his right standing before God, is "like filthy rags" or a filthy garment (Isaiah 64:6). You cannot earn salvation through what you do or what you have accomplished. Paul counted everything he ever did before Christ as loss so he could gain the excellent knowledge of Christ Jesus our Lord (Philippians 3:8).

Now let us go to James 2:14-26 where James informs us that "faith without works is dead". He tells us that Abraham was justified by works along with his faith. He later tells us that we can plainly see that a man is not justified by faith only. He concludes that chapter with a comparison. Without the spirit inside, the body is dead; without works, faith is dead.

Paul even relates to this back in Ephesians 2:10 where we were earlier, and he concludes that even though we are saved by grace and not of works yet he lets the church know that we are his workmanship, created in Christ Jesus to do good works that God ordained that we should walk in them. Does Paul now contradict what he told the Romans? Did James contradict what Paul said to the church at Rome? Which is it? Are we saved by faith and by works also, or is it by faith alone?

As I stated earlier in the book, if you listen to some men or the "Man of God" you will hear one thing but if you listen to the Word of God you will hear another. Remember, we must all stand before the judgment seat of Christ. We must all give an account of what we have done. Let's see what God's Word tells us regarding works and its relation to faith. We will see that our works prior to our faith in Christ do not count, but that our works after our faith in Christ can make us complete and grant us an entrance into the kingdom of heaven. Sounds like heresy to most, but what does God's Word says about it?

Let's go to Revelation and the letters that our Lord Jesus wrote to the churches. These letters are written to believers in Jesus Christ - people who have faith in Christ and believe that it is by grace we are saved through faith and not of works. As a matter of fact, the first letter is written to the church at Ephesus. This is the very church that Paul wrote to. The Lord Jesus tells them that he knows their works. He compliments them on some of their works, but then he has something against them. Anytime the Lord says he has something against you, I would listen very carefully to what he is about to say. Eternity depends on it. He told them they had left their first love. He went on to tell them to remember from where they fell and to do the first works or else he would remove them from their place with him. Do works matter after you get saved? Do works have any bearing on your relationship with Christ? According to the Lord if they did not repent they were being removed. Who was being removed? The body of Christ at Ephesus was being removed. Notice he said they fell and then told them to repent.

Look at the letter to the church in Sardis in Revelation chapter 3. The Lord told them that they have a name that declares they are alive but in reality they are dead. How many churches today declare they are alive but in reality they are dead? He told these groups of believers to watch and make strong the things that remain that are also ready to die because he did not find their works complete before God. He went on to say that they should remember how they received and heard, and then they were to repent. He said if they did not watch he would come on them as a thief in the night. He concluded with that church body that if they did not overcome, then he would blot their names out of the Book of Life. What do you mean blot their name out of the Book of Life? I thought your works have nothing to do with your salvation? I thought once you got saved you were always saved? Why was he telling this to believers? Shouldn't he be speaking this to sinners instead of to believers?

The Lord told this church to watch. That word watch means to stand guard. Why stand guard waiting for the Lord? Is there a chance I might miss him? Is there a chance I might not make it when he comes? How can that be if I am saved already? What am I watching for? The Lord told the disciples in Matthew 24 to watch and be ready. Why? Because you do not know what hour your Lord is coming. Notice he said you do not know what hour "your Lord" is coming, so watch and be ready or you may not make it. The word ready means to be prepared. Do you mean there is more to it than just getting saved? Do you mean I have to do something else to be prepared? He told that church in Revelation 3 to repent and to get the stains out of their garment. The church is to be spotless. Someone said we are spotless through the blood of Jesus. His blood has cleansed us from all sin. That is true, but why did the Lord tell this church that if they did not get the stains out of their garments then he would blot their names out of the Book of Life?

This church evidently had believers who had defiled their garments after they became believers, and that is why their works were not complete before God, and that is why they had a chance of having their names blotted out. Paul wrote to the

Ephesians in chapter 5 that the Lord gave himself for us, the church, so that he could set it apart and clean it with the washing of water by his Word. He wants to present it to himself a church without spot or wrinkle, and it should be holy and without marks or stains. Evidently, according to these passages of scriptures, stains can be on believers' garments after they have become believers. What stains are on your garment? Is it the stain of unforgiving? Is there someone in your life you have not forgiven? Are you not set apart for the Lord to do his will? Are you greedy and going after money? Are you full of pride and putting yourself above others? Are you having sex outside of marriage or are you walking in adultery? How about lying, or stealing, or cheating? We could go on and on and on, but the fact remains that we must have a clean garment before the Lord comes or we stand a good chance of our names being blotted out of his Book of Life. For many ministers, this throws a roadblock to much of their preaching. It is not easy to confront a congregation that they may not be ready to meet the Lord. It could cost ministers thousands of dollars if they confront people with things that may make them leave their church. After all, they can just go to the church down the street that does not teach this kind of Word. How easy it is, as Paul declares to the churches, that some can handle the Word of God deceitfully (2 Corinthians 4:2). They avoid this kind of preaching for fear of losing their congregation or the money that is being brought in.

Let us look at the Laodecian church in Revelation 3. The Lord wrote them and told them that he knew their works. It must matter what kind of works we are doing because throughout all of these letters the Lord refers to the works of his body, no matter if they were good or bad. He told this group of believers that they were not hot or cold, but lukewarm. In that day, the church of Laodicea was near a city called Hierapolis which had an abundance of hot water, and the waters were known for their medicinal qualities. The city of Colossae was known for its pure cold water which had many uses as well. The city of Laodicea had to receive water by aqueducts and by the time the water arrived it was lukewarm and very nauseating to the taste. In other words, the water was not good for any use. That is what the terms meant when the Lord spoke to the church there. He told them they were not of any use according to their works. Their works could have been cold or hot to provide something pleasing in the eyes of the Lord, but they were not. He then told them that since they were lukewarm he was going to vomit them out of his mouth. In other words, they were no longer going to be in him. The Word of God tells us in John 15:6 that if we do not abide in Christ, then we will be cast forth as a branch and then later burned. This

church no longer would abide in Christ because of
their works being lukewarm. The love of our Lord
through all of these letters is confirmed in the letter
to this church. He told them that he was rebuking
them and correcting them because he loved them.
He gives everyone time to repent and turn back to
the Lord and to do what they should be doing. In
other words, he gives them a chance to do the works
he has called them to do. He told this church body
that he stood at the door of their heart, knocking on
that door. He was knocking through the words he
was speaking to them. If they would open that door
of their heart by obeying his words, then he would
come in and begin to eat with them and fellowship
with them again. Evidently he was not in the heart
of these believers any longer if he had to knock of the
door of their hearts to let him back in.

Paul warned the Corinthian Church in 1
Corinthians 10 of the danger of doing works that are
not acceptable before God because they could miss
the kingdom of heaven like the children of Israel
before them. Why would Paul warn those who were
already believers? He wanted to make sure they did
not follow the examples of the children of Israel. If
they were saved already, then what difference would
it make? After all, the Lord has washed away all of
our sins with his precious blood. Surely if we had
one little spot or one little wrinkle the Lord would
understand. It is sad to say, but that is what is

taught in many churches today. That is why the Lord said many will come to him in that day and say Lord, Lord when they were not actually doing the will of God.

What about what Paul said when he told the Corinthian Church (1 Corinthians 3) that their works may be burned up but they themselves would be saved. Paul told them that they were a carnal group of believers. There were divisions among them. They were trying to form denominations, just like we have today. One was of Paul, another was of Peter, and another was of Apollos. He went on to explain in chapter 3 that these men were only ministers appointed by God so the people could learn about the Lord and believed on Him. One of them planted and one of them watered, but God gave the increase. The one who plants and the one who waters are nothing. I hope that hits your heart hard to understand that ministers are nothing! These men and women are gifts given to us to lead us to Christ. We are to worship the gift-giver, not the gift. Paul went on to say that these ministers are laborers, working together to build the house of God. One lays the foundation and others built other parts of the house. The ones who do the works of building on the foundation of Jesus Christ will have their works tested by fire. Some will be rewarded and others will have their works burned up, but they will all still be saved. This is all about ministers and their works of preaching and teaching. It is about building the body of Christ. He is not referring here to works of an individual life. The workers of iniquity that were told to depart (Matthew 7) were preaching the Word, casting out devils, and many wonderful works. According to Mark 16, those are the signs that follow believers. However, in this case, they had to depart from him because of their individual lifestyle of living in iniquity. Just because a man is preaching the Gospel and casting out devils and doing many wonderful works does not mean he is living a right lifestyle. According to the Lord, he could still be living in iniquity. They are known by their fruits, not their preaching. That is why the Lord said in John 15 that if any man is in him but does not bear fruit, he will be cut off and burned. Paul concludes in 1 Corinthians 3 that we are the temple of God and any man, even ministers, that defiles this temple will be destroyed by God.

If we are in Christ, we are a new creation (2 Corinthians 5:17). Evidently the believers at the Laodicean Church were no longer in Christ due to their works. He was going to vomit them out unless they repented and purchased the things he told them to purchase. They had to purchase something from him in order to get back to doing the works he called them to do. In verse 17, it sounds like the Church today. We are increased in goods and have need of nothing. The Lord told them to buy gold that has been tested in the fire so they can get the impurities out of their life that is causing them to be lukewarm, to get a white garment signifying to be pure before God, and to put ointment on their eyes so they can see the error of their ways and repent.

The Lord loves his body and wants to present it to himself without spots or wrinkles. Peter reminds us to be diligent so we can be spotless and blameless (2 Peter 3:14). Paul warns us in Titus 1:16 that may people will profess that they know God, but in their works they will actually deny him. Our works are crucial – they can deny God! He later comments in Titus chapter 3:7-8 that even though we are justified by grace and believe in God, that we should also be careful to maintain good works. In Hebrews 6:9-10 we learn that there are things that are supposed to accompany salvation. This group of believers had done works to accompany their salvation. They had ministered to the saints as their work and labor of love toward the Lord's name. What is pure religion before God? The term "religious" has become a negative term, indicating legalistic requirements for hair length, clothing style, adornments, and such. We are given the definition of pure religion in James 1:27. He tells us it is to visit the fatherless and widows in their affliction and to keep ourselves unspotted from this world. From what I have observed, there is very little church ministry toward orphans and widows.

They are "thrown a bone" now and then, but the majority of ministry does not go to these types of individuals.

In the Lord's message in Matthew 24, he tells his disciples to watch and be ready because they do not know when their Lord will return. This was in reference to the fact that he was coming back and that his children should be watching and be ready. In chapter 25 he gives an example of what can happen to his servants if they are not ready. He gave his servants talents in verses 14-15. He gave them to his children so they could use them while he was away. When he returned, he expected them to have a return on his investment. In other words, they needed to have made a profit of some kind in regards to what he gave them. In verses 24-30, the servant did not make a return on the talent he was given. Notice that this is a servant and Jesus is his Lord. Notice also that he called this servant unprofitable. This believer in Jesus did not do what his Lord told him to do, and according to the Word of the Lord, he will be thrown into outer darkness. Do you mean a servant of the Lord can be thrown out of the kingdom? Apparently so! We must be ready when our Lord returns. We must be doing what he tells us to do.

We could go on and on with God's Word in reference to the reason good works should follow salvation, but I will leave you with only one more. In 2 Peter chapter 1 the Apostle Peter tells the believers that if they have the good works of self-control, patience, godliness, and especially love, then they will be fruitful in knowing the Lord Jesus Christ. He then said that if they lacked these things, they are blind and have forgotten that they were purged from their old sins. It is of utmost importance that we make our calling in Christ sure by doing these good works of self-control, patience, godliness, and love so we will never fall. If we do these things, then an entrance into the kingdom of our Lord and Savior Jesus Christ will be given to us. According to Peter, these things should follow our conversion and if they are not abounding in our life then we might not get an entrance into God's kingdom.

These truths have been kept from the body of Christ and they have been misled into thinking that all they have to do is get saved and "live happily ever after". They have not been told that they have to die and no longer exist – that God is now working in them to will and to do of his good pleasure. I understand more and more why the Lord said that many will come to him in that day and say Lord, Lord but not get an entrance into his kingdom. I pray you take heed to these words and, if you are found not conforming to them, that you repent and ask the Lord to forgive you and begin to walk in them fresh and new. He is standing at your heart knocking through these words. Will you let him in where he once was? Will you let his will be done and not yours? He loves you and waits for you.

WHAT IS LACKING?

In Mark 10 there was a rich young ruler who came running to Jesus and knelt before him, asking what he should do to inherit eternal life. This is the question most people have asked all of their life and what this book has addressed. This man happened to ask the one who gives eternal life and who knows everything. He is the living Word of God and knows all things. Jesus told the man that he already knew the commandments and the Lord went on to repeat them. The man responded that he had kept the commandments since he was young. The Lord looked at him and loved him and told him he lacked one thing. What a compassionate Savior we have! He loves this whole world and just waits patiently for them to come to him asking for eternal life. He told this man he lacked one thing. He told him to sell all of his possessions and give them to the poor, and take up his cross, and come and follow him. The rich young ruler went away sad because he was very rich. The Lord told the disciples that it is very hard for those that trust in riches to enter into heaven.

What one thing is keeping you from having eternal life? Do you trust in riches? Do you have your trust in anything more than the Lord? Is there someone in your life you cannot forgive? Is there prejudice in your heart towards others? Did someone do something to you in the past that you cannot get over and you hold it against them? Are people living a certain lifestyle that causes you to hate them? Are you living a certain lifestyle that you do not want to give up? The list could go on and on, but the question remains - what thing are you lacking in your life that keeps you from eternal life?

This young man was keeping the commandments of God, but still lacked one thing. He was doing what God's Word was telling him but he still lacked one thing. Every individual must examine their own heart to see what one thing is keeping them from having eternal life. I have mentioned many times about the letters the Lord sent to the churches in the book of Revelation. In Revelation 2:4 the Lord stated he had something against that church. They had left their first love. Is that the one thing you lack? In Revelation 2:20 the Lord said he had a few things against that church. They were allowing false doctrine to be taught in their church. Is that the one thing you are lacking in? Are you believing in false doctrine and practicing it?

In all of these cases, the people that were lacking the one thing were going to miss heaven and not have eternal life. Imagine going through your whole life and only lacking just one thing that causes you to miss heaven. I remember hearing a preacher when I was only one year old in the Lord. He was trying to ease the conscience of everyone by telling them that a little sin in their life was okay because the Lord understands that no one is perfect. We have allowed that kind of doctrine and teaching in the church for years. We no longer give an account of what we do before God. We only give an account before man. We call good evil and evil good. The current message is that everyone sins a little but God understands. We believe that denominations are good, but God's Word says just the opposite. The Lord told us that a little leaven makes the whole lump bad. You cannot have one thing lacking in your life before the living God but still make heaven.

I encourage you to open your heart and examine it. Make sure it is pure before God and that you have forsaken everything and are following the Lord. The Lord told all of those that had something lacking to forsake everything and follow him. In other words, repent or turn away from the one thing you lack and follow him now. Do not let that one thing keep you from heaven. Do not allow man to keep you bound in his doctrine and teaching when it is the opposite of the Lord's doctrine and teaching.

This book was written to let you know God loves you so much that he is reaching out to make sure you are ready when he comes. He wants you prepared for that great day when he comes to take his church away. He wants his bride to be without spot and without wrinkle. He wants his body cleansed and sanctified for his return. The Apostle Paul stated in 1 Corinthians 14:1 that we are to make the love of God our great quest and aim in this life. If you are found in love when the Lord returns, you will not be lacking anything. Make sure every day to keep your eyes on love. By doing so, we keep our eyes on God who is love. He is the way, the truth, and the life, and no one can get to the Father but by love.

I pray the Lord will open your eyes to these truths and that you will be found in him and in his love when he returns.

ABOUT THE AUTHOR

Bill was born and raised in Baltimore, Maryland into a large Italian Catholic family. At the age of 20, he had a supernatural experience that changed his life forever. He was born again just as the Lord Jesus said in the Gospel of John, chapter 3.

He was led by the Spirit of God to move to Texas shortly thereafter. Since graduating from the Word of Faith Bible College in 1979, he has taught and preached God's Word for over 30 years.

Almighty God led him to be an Associate Pastor at Trinity Community Church in Bedford, Texas where he fed the Body of Christ God's Holy Word for over 20 years.

He and his wife, Ranell, have now begun a new work for the Lord called A Life Of Love Ministries.

www.ingramcontent.com/pod-product-compliance
Lightning Source LLC
Chambersburg PA
CBHW031325040426
42443CB00005B/216